KS2
Success
SATs

Level 5

Maths

LEARN AND PRACTISE

Paul Broadbent

Contents

Understanding shape

Measuring

Handling data

Glossary

Answers

Word problems

Answering problems

If you have a word problem to solve, it may help to follow these stages.

Peter uses 500g of flour each day to make bread. A 1.5kg bag of flour costs him 86p. How much will he spend on flour to make bread for 12 days?

1 Read the problem.

Try to picture the problem and imagine going through it in real life.

2 Sort out the calculations.

500g × 12 is the amount of flour he uses. Divide this by 1.5kg to work out the number of bags. Multiply 86p by the number of bags needed.

3 Answer the calculations.

500 × 12 = 6000g = 6kg
6 ÷ 1.5 = 4 bags
86 × 4 = 344

4 Answer the problem.

Look back at the question – what is it asking?
The cost of flour for bread for 12 days is £3.44.

Multi-step problems

Word problems can have different numbers of calculations to answer before you reach the final answer.

Two-step problems
A computer costs £985. It has a 10% discount in a sale. What is the new sale price?

Step 1   10% of £985 is £98.50.

Step 2   985.00
            − 98.50
            886.50   The computer costs £886.50.

Three-step problems
Gemma bought a book of 45 stamps. She used $\frac{1}{5}$ of them on Monday and used 17 more on Tuesday. How many stamps does she have left?

Step 1   Step 2   Step 3

$\frac{1}{5}$ of 45 = 9   45 − 9 = 36   36 − 17 = 19

Gemma has 19 stamps left.

Answering problems

1   Gemma saved £100 to spend on some clothes. She spent $\frac{2}{5}$ of her
    money in one shop. How much money did she have left?   £ [ ]

2   A flight had a baggage allowance of 32kg. A passenger had two
    cases and when one was placed on the scales it weighed 19.65kg.
    What is the maximum weight allowed for his other case?   [ ] kg

3   In a survey of 140 children, 15% of the children asked said that they
    had watched the news on television the previous evening.
    How many children in total had watched the news?   [ ]

4   These boxes are stored on a tray. Calculate the largest number
    of boxes that will fit on the tray, with no overlapping or stacked boxes.

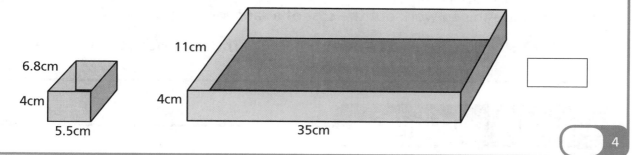

6.8cm

4cm

5.5cm

11cm

4cm

35cm

[ ]

4

Multi-step problems

1   278 people went to a school concert. They each paid a 75p
    entrance fee and 50% of them bought programmes for 40p.
    How much money was paid altogether?   £ [ ]

2   Circle the offer that sells bread rolls at the lowest individual price for a roll:

    Bag of 12 rolls: £2.24.

    Offer: Buy 1 bag, get 1 bag half price.

    Bag of 6 rolls: £1.35.

    Offer: Buy 2 bags, get 3rd bag free.

3   A pack of six golf balls, including the packaging, weighs a total
    of 298g. The packaging weighs 40g. What is the total weight of
    the pack if two of the balls are taken out?   [ ] g

4   Sam is having a party and needs enough chocolate bars for
    39 people. He buys packs of choc bars that cost £2.39 for 5 bars.
    How much will it cost to buy enough packs so
    that each person has a choc bar?   £ [ ]

4

TOTAL MARKS [8]

Problem-solving

Reasoning

If you need to think carefully about a way to solve a problem, you are likely to be using reasoning skills to make sense of it. Some maths questions look simple, but involve a lot of thought. It may help to explain the problem to someone else, describing the way you could try to solve it.

A drink and a sandwich together cost £2.55.

Two drinks and a sandwich together cost £3.45.

What is the cost of a sandwich?

To answer this, work out the cost of a drink (the **difference** between the two prices), then use this to work out the cost of a sandwich.

£3.45 – £2.55 = 90p   £2.55 – 90p = £1.65   The sandwich costs £1.65.

Finding all possibilities

These types of problems often have lots of choices of answers and the skill is finding the correct one. Work systematically, making lists of all possible answers to find the right one.

A group of 12 people book a trip to an aquarium. It costs £8, but some of the group pay only £5, as they are over 65 years old. The 12 people pay a total of £81. How many over-65s are in the group?

Draw a table to help you answer this.

Number of people	£8 entrance	£5 entrance
1	£8	£5
2	£16	£10
3	£24	£15
4	£32	£20
5	£40	**£25**
6	£48	£30
7	**£56**	£35

7 × £8 and 5 × £5 totals £81, so there are 5 over-65s in the group.

Look for a total of 12 people with a combined cost of £81.

Key words   difference

Reasoning

A and B each stand for a different number. A = 12.
What is the value of B for each of these?

1 A + A = A + B + B

2 A² + A = B + B

3 A (A + A) = B + A

4 A drink and a hot-dog together cost £1.25. Two drinks and a hot-dog together cost £1.80. How much does a hot-dog cost? p

5 If you add a 3-digit number to a 3-digit number you cannot get a 5-digit number. Is this true or false? Explain how you know.

_____

 Reasoning is all about thinking things through. Read the questions a few times so that you can sort out a strategy to answer the problem.

Top Tip

5

Finding all possibilities

1 Circle the two consecutive numbers that give a product of 2256.

27   28   29   37   38   39   47   48   49

2 X and Y are two different whole numbers.
X + Y = 2000   X is 450 greater than Y.

X = ▢   Y = ▢

3 A necklace has white beads weighing 11 grams each and black beads weighing 15 grams each. There are 12 beads altogether and the total weight of the beads is 160g. How many black beads are there? ▢

4 An isosceles triangle has a perimeter of 23cm. One of its sides is 8.4cm. What are possible lengths of the other two sides? ▢ cm and ▢ cm

5 Which three prime numbers multiply to make 231? ▢ × ▢ × ▢ = 231

5

Rules and patterns

Number sequences

A **sequence** is a list of numbers which usually have a pattern. You can often find the pattern or rule in a sequence by looking at the difference between the numbers.

What is the next number in the sequence?   42   27   12   –3   –18   ____

Each number is 15 less than the previous one, so the next number is –33.
The rule is 'subtract 15'.

Formulae and equations

A **formula** (plural is formulae) uses letters or words to give a rule.

What is the rule for this sequence of numbers?

A	1	2	3	4	5	n
B	4	7	10	13	16	?

Look at the relationship between the pairs of numbers. The numbers in row A are multiplied by 3 and then 1 is added to make each of the numbers in row B. So for n, the formula is $3n + 1$. You can use this to find any number in the pattern. What is the 15th number in the sequence? $3 \times 15 + 1 = 46$.

Equations have symbols or letters instead of numbers in a calculation.

$\blacksquare + 2 = 15$ $4\blacktriangle - 5 = 19$ $3y + 9 = 24$

You need to work out what the symbol or letter stands for, so use the numbers given to help you.

 Top Tip *Equations need to stay balanced. If you add or take away a number from one side, do the same to the other side, so the equation stays the same. It's a good way of working out the letter.*

Try working it out step-by-step. $3y + 9 = 24$

1   You want y on one side of the equation and the numbers on the other. Subtract 9 from both sides. If it were –9, you would add 9 to both sides.
$3y = 24 - 9$ $3y = 15$

2   Say the equation as a sentence: 3 times something makes 15. So $y = 5$.

3   Test it with the original equation: $(3 \times 5) + 9 = 24$.

 Key words   sequence   formula   equation

Number sequences

Write the pattern or rule for each sequence for one mark. Then underline yes or no for each question for a second mark.

1   –6   –1   4   9   14   the rule is _____

Will 99 be in this sequence?   yes / no

2   –8   –5   –2   1   4   the rule is _____

Will 30 be in this sequence?   yes / no

3   20   14   8   2   – 4   the rule is _____

Will –20 be in this sequence?   yes / no

4   11   7   3   –1   –5   the rule is _____

Will –21 be in this sequence?   yes / no

5   –52   –22   8   38   68   the rule is _____

Will 180 be in this sequence?   yes / no

10

Formulae and equations

Work out the value of each letter.

1 3h + 2 = 26 ☐   **2** 4y – 5 = 11 ☐   **3** 2r + 1 = 15 ☐

4   Callum made a shape pattern with counters. The table shows the number of counters he used for each shape.

Shape number	1	2	3	4	n
Counters	2	6	10	14	?

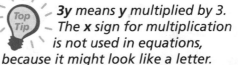

Tick the correct formula for this shape pattern.

3n – 1 ☐   2n + 2 ☐   4n – 2 ☐   5n – 3 ☐   3n + 1 ☐

5   Callum uses 58 counters to make a shape in this pattern.

What is its shape number? ☐

3y means *y* multiplied by 3. The **x** sign for multiplication is not used in equations, because it might look like a letter.

5

TOTAL MARKS 15

Comparing and ordering

Ordering decimals

Putting decimals in order is just like putting whole numbers in order – you need to look carefully at the value of each digit.

These are the times for the women's 50m freestyle swimming final at the last Olympics. What order did they finish the race in?

Swimmer	Time (seconds)
Michelle Engelsman, Australia	25.06
Kara Lynn Joyce, United States	25.00
Inge de Bruijn, Netherlands	24.58
Libby Lenton, Australia	24.91
Therese Alshammar, Sweden	24.93
Malia Metella, France	24.89

Write them out one under the other.

25.06
25.00
24.58
24.91
24.93
24.89

Compare the digits from left to right, re-ordering the numbers so that the smallest number is first.

24.58
24.89
24.91
24.93
25.00
25.06

Top Tip

Remember to line up the decimal points.

Negative numbers

Positive numbers are above zero and negative numbers are below zero.

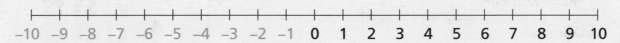

We can compare numbers by looking at their positions on the number line.

Look at the differences between these pairs of temperatures.

inside	outside	difference
6°C	–4°C	10°C
12°C	–7°C	19°C
–1°C	–9°C	8°C

Key words   digit   negative number

Ordering decimals

Use the four digits and the decimal point to answer these questions.
There must be one digit in front of the decimal point.

| 4 | 8 | 9 | 1 | • |

1   What is the largest decimal number you can make?   ___ • ___ ___ ___

2   What is the smallest decimal number you can make?   ___ • ___ ___ ___

3   Make a decimal number as near as possible to 9.   ___ • ___ ___ ___

4   Make a decimal number between 1.5 and 1.9.   ___ • ___ ___ ___

5   Write all the decimal numbers you have made in order, from smallest to largest.

smallest   **largest**

5

Negative numbers

What is the difference in temperature between these pairs of thermometers?

1   _____ °

2      _____ °

3   _____ °

4   Circle the two numbers with a difference of 18.

   −9   −7   8   7   13   −11

5   Write these temperatures in order, starting with the lowest.

   8.5°C   6°C   −8°C   −4°C   −11°C   1.5°C

lowest   **highest**

5

Fractions

Equivalent fractions

Equivalent fractions have different numerators and denominators, but are worth the same value.

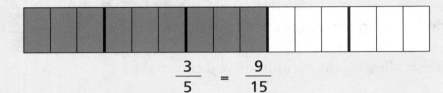

$$\frac{3}{5} = \frac{9}{15}$$

A fraction can be changed into its equivalent by multiplying the numerator and denominator by the same amount.

$$3 \times 3 = 9 \qquad 5 \times 3 = 15$$

You can reduce a fraction to an equivalent fraction by dividing the top and bottom by the highest common factor – the biggest number that will divide into both.

$$\frac{18}{24} = \frac{3}{4} \qquad 18 \div 6 = 3 \qquad 24 \div 6 = 4$$

$\frac{3}{4}$ is a fraction in its lowest terms, or simplest form.

Comparing fractions

If fractions have the same denominator, they are easy to compare.

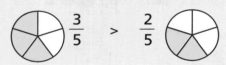

$$\frac{3}{5} > \frac{2}{5}$$

To compare fractions with different denominators, change them to equivalent fractions with a common denominator – the same denominator.

Which is the larger fraction, $\frac{2}{3}$ or $\frac{3}{4}$?

Find the equivalent fractions to $\frac{2}{3}$ and $\frac{3}{4}$ that have a common denominator.

$$\frac{2}{3} = \frac{4}{6} = \frac{6}{9} = \frac{8}{12} \qquad \frac{3}{4} = \frac{6}{8} = \frac{9}{12}$$

$\frac{9}{12}$ is larger than $\frac{8}{12}$, so $\frac{3}{4}$ is larger than $\frac{2}{3}$.

Top Tip *You can also compare fractions by changing them to decimals.*

Key words numerator   denominator   highest common factor
common denominator

Equivalent fractions

Write the fraction in its simplest form for the shaded part of each shape.

1

2

3

4

5

5

Comparing fractions

Look at these number cards.

$$\boxed{3} \quad \boxed{2} \quad \boxed{8} \quad \boxed{7} \quad \boxed{5}$$

1 Use two of the number cards to complete this: $\dfrac{\square}{\square} > \dfrac{1}{2}$

2 Use four of the number cards to complete this: $\dfrac{\square}{\square} < \dfrac{\square}{\square}$

3 Which is larger, $\frac{2}{3}$ or $\frac{4}{5}$? Explain how you know.

_____

4 Write a fraction that lies between $\frac{1}{4}$ and $\frac{3}{8}$. $\dfrac{\square}{\square}$

5 Write a fraction that could complete this: $\dfrac{3}{5} > \dfrac{\square}{\square} > \dfrac{1}{3}$

5

TOTAL MARKS 10

Fractions, decimals, percentages

Percentages and fractions

Percentages are simply fractions out of 100 – that is what per cent means: out of 100.

% is the percentage sign.

In a tile pattern of 100 tiles, 25 are red.
25% of the tiles are red, which is $\frac{1}{4}$ of the tiles.

Another tile pattern of 20 tiles has 5 red tiles. This also means 25% of the tiles are red.

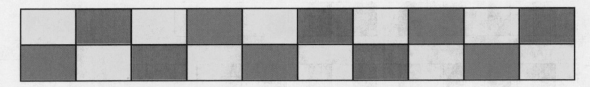

To change fractions to percentages, make them out of 100. This means you need to find an **equivalent fraction** with the denominator 100.

$\frac{3}{5}$ is equivalent to $\frac{60}{100}$, so $\frac{3}{5}$ = 60%.

To change per cent to fraction, write the percentage as a fraction out of 100 and then reduce to its lowest terms.

40% is $\frac{40}{100}$, which is the same as $\frac{2}{5}$.

5% is $\frac{5}{100}$, which is the same as $\frac{1}{20}$.

Top Tip
If you find it easier, write the fraction as a decimal and then multiply by 100.
$\frac{3}{4}$ is 0.75, which is the same as 75%.

Equivalent values

It is a good idea to memorise these. Cover up different boxes and work out the covered amounts.

Decimals	0.1	0.2	0.3	0.4	0.5	0.6	0.7	0.8	0.9	0.25	0.75
Fractions	$\frac{1}{10}$	$\frac{1}{5}$	$\frac{3}{10}$	$\frac{2}{5}$	$\frac{1}{2}$	$\frac{3}{5}$	$\frac{7}{10}$	$\frac{4}{5}$	$\frac{9}{10}$	$\frac{1}{4}$	$\frac{3}{4}$
Percent	10%	20%	30%	40%	50%	60%	70%	80%	90%	25%	75%

Key words   percentage   equivalent fraction

Percentages and fractions

These are Josh's maths test scores as marks out of a total. Convert each of the scores to percentages.

1 7 out of 10 = [ ] %

2 16 out of 20 = [ ] %

3 38 out of 50 = [ ] %

4 20 out of 25 = [ ] %

[4]

Equivalent values

Write the missing numbers to complete these.

1 $\dfrac{1}{\boxed{}}$ = 0.[ ] = 50%

2 $\dfrac{\boxed{}}{4}$ = 0.25 = [ ] %

3 $\dfrac{1}{20}$ = 0.[ ] = [ ] %

4 $\dfrac{2}{\boxed{}}$ = 0.4 = [ ] %

5 $\dfrac{17}{50}$ = 0.[ ] = [ ] %

6 $\dfrac{7}{\boxed{}}$ = 0.7 = [ ] %

7 $\dfrac{\boxed{}}{100}$ = 0.09 = [ ] %

8 $\dfrac{11}{\boxed{}}$ = 0.44 = [ ] %

Write <, > or = to make each statement true.

9 25%   [ ]   0.25

10 0.2   [ ]   20%

11 0.75   [ ]   57%

12 4%   [ ]   0.4

13 8%   [ ]   0.8

14 0.1   [ ]   10%

15 7%   [ ]   0.07

16 $\dfrac{2}{5}$ [ ]   0.4

If you are asked to convert a percentage to a decimal, remember that it will always be less than 1.

[16]

TOTAL MARKS [20]

Ratio

Ratio

Ratio is used to compare one amount with another.

What is the ratio of green to orange tiles?

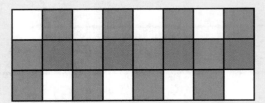

There are 4 green tiles and 12 orange tiles. For every 1 green tile, there are 3 orange tiles. The ratio of green to orange is 1 to 3, or 1:3.

This ratio stays the same for different amounts:

Green	1	2	3	4	5	6
Orange	3	6	9	12	15	18

How many green tiles are needed if 60 tiles are used in this pattern?

The proportion of tiles that are green is 1 in every 6, or $\frac{1}{6}$.

This means that in a set of 60 tiles, 10 would be green.

Top Tip *Ratios are a bit like fractions – they can both be simplified by finding the highest common factors. For example, in a class of 16 boys and 12 girls, the ratio of boys to girls is 16:12. This can be simplified by dividing by 4 to give a ratio of 4:3.*

Direct proportion

Two quantities are in direct proportion when they increase or decrease in the same ratio. For example, if 3 pens cost 90p, what is the cost of 15 pens?

This is 5 times the number of pens, so it is five times the price. 90p × 5 = £4.50.

Scale drawings and maps are examples of ways we use direct proportion.

This car is drawn at a scale of 50:1. The drawing is 4.6cm long. How long is the actual car?

4.6cm × 50 = 230cm = 2.3m

 Key words　　　　ratio　　proportion

Ratio

1   Ali shares out 24 sweets. He gives Sophie 1 sweet for every 3 he takes. How many sweets does Sophie get? □

2   Hannah puts some tulips, daffodils and carnations in a vase. For every one tulip, she uses three daffodils and four carnations. She uses 40 flowers altogether. How many daffodils does she use? □

3   Daniel mixes 1 litre of white paint with every 4 litres of green paint. He needs 20 litres of paint altogether. How many litres of green paint will he need? □

4   Robert pours 1 carton of orange juice and 1 carton of cranberry juice into a jug. He wants only half as much orange juice as cranberry juice in the mixture. What should he pour into his jug now? _____

5   An 80g snack bar has 80% oats and 20% fruit. What is the ratio of oats to fruit in a bar, in its simplest form? _____

5

Direct proportion

In this recipe the amount of each ingredient is given as a proportion of the total weight.

1   Write the weight of each ingredient into the recipe.

2   Using this recipe, how many grams of butter would be needed for a 900g cake? _____

3   Here is a rectangle with six identical shaded squares in it. The width is 4.5cm. What is the length of the rectangle?

_____

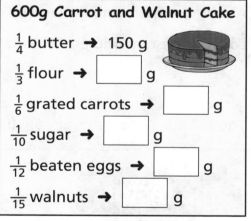

600g Carrot and Walnut Cake

$\frac{1}{4}$ butter → 150 g

$\frac{1}{3}$ flour → [ ] g

$\frac{1}{6}$ grated carrots → [ ] g

$\frac{1}{10}$ sugar → [ ] g

$\frac{1}{12}$ beaten eggs → [ ] g

$\frac{1}{15}$ walnuts → [ ] g

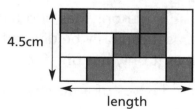

4.5cm

length

4   Six toy cars cost a total of £4.50. What is the cost of ten cars? _____

5   A 1.2 litre jug of lemon squash is mixed in the proportion of $\frac{1}{10}$ fruit juice to $\frac{9}{10}$ water. How much juice is in the jug when it is half full? _____

5

TOTAL MARKS (10

Multiples and factors

Factors

Factors are numbers that will divide exactly into other numbers. It is useful to put factors of numbers into pairs:

Factors of 30 ➜ (1,30), (2,15), (3,10), (5,6) = 8 factors

Factors of 45 ➜ (1,45), (3,15), (5,9) = 6 factors

If you look at the factors of 30 and 45, there are some factors that are the same for both numbers. The numbers 1, 3, 5 and 15 are common factors of 30 and 45.

15 is the largest number which is a common factor of 30 and 45, which means that the **Highest Common Factor** (written as HCF) of 30 and 45 is 15.

Top Tip — *Highest common factors are used to simplify equivalent fractions. For example, $\frac{32}{56}$ can be simplified to $\frac{4}{7}$ by dividing by the HCF of 32 and 56, which is 8.*

Multiples

A **multiple** is a number made by multiplying together two other numbers.

Look at these multiples of 6 and 8.

Multiples of 6 ➜ 6, 12, 18, **24**, 30, 36 …

Multiples of 8 ➜ 8, 16, **24**, 32, 40, 48 …

The **Lowest Common Multiple** (LCM) of 6 and 8 is 24.

Prime factors

A **prime number** only has two factors: 1 and itself. For example, 23 is a prime number, as it can only be divided by 1 and 23. The number 1 is **not** a prime number, as it only has one factor.

The **prime factors** of a number are all those factors of the number which are prime numbers.

All the factors of 28 are 1, 2, 4, 7, 14 and 28. The prime factors of 28 are 2 and 7.

 Key words

| factor | highest common factor | multiple |
| lowest common multiple | prime number | prime factor |

Factors

List the common factors for each of these. Underline the HCF for each set.

1 Common factors of 12 and 42. _____

2 Common factors of 15 and 45. _____

3 Common factors of 14 and 42. _____

4 Common factors of 36, 42 and 48. _____

5 Common factors of 12, 24 and 30. _____

5

Multiples

Write the numbers **2**, **3**, **4**, **5**, **6** or **9** to complete these statements.

1 92 is a multiple of ☐ and ☐.

2 117 is a multiple of ☐ and ☐.

3 280 is a multiple of ☐, ☐ and ☐.

4 84 is a multiple of ☐, ☐, ☐ and ☐.

5 432 is a multiple of ☐, ☐, ☐, ☐ and ☐.

6 9180 is a multiple of ☐, ☐, ☐, ☐, ☐ and ☐.

7 What is the lowest common multiple of 9 and 4? ☐

 *Top Tip* To work out multiples of different numbers, use rules of divisibility. e.g. 92 cannot be divided by 3, because the digits of 92 do not total 3, 6 or 9. So 92 is not a multiple of 3.

7

Prime factors

Choose any of these factors to complete the multiplications.

3   4   5   7   11   13

1 ☐ × ☐ × ☐ = 84   **3** ☐ × ☐ × ☐ = 715

2 ☐ × ☐ × ☐ = 132

3

Estimating answers

Rounding decimals

Rounding decimals makes them easier to work with. For example, this bag weighs 6.372 kilograms.

This is very exact and you probably only need to know that it is about 6kg, or if you want to be a little more accurate, it weighs about 6.4kg.

Decimals are usually rounded to the nearest whole number or nearest tenth.

Rounding to the nearest whole number:

- Look at the tenths digit.

- If it is 5 or more, round up to the next whole number.

- If it is less than 5, the units digit stays the same.

16.5 rounds up to 17.

7.48 rounds down to 7.

Rounding to the nearest tenth:

- Look at the hundredths digit.

- If it is 5 or more, round up to the next tenth.

- If it is less than 5, the tenths digit stays the same.

13.77 rounds up to 13.8.

4.639 rounds down to 4.6.

> **Top Tip** *This is called rounding to a number of decimal places. If you have a question that asks you to round to 1 decimal place, it means round the number to the nearest tenth. If you are asked to round to 2 decimal places, it means round to the nearest hundredth.*

Approximate answers

When you add, subtract, multiply or divide large numbers or decimals, it is always a good idea to estimate an approximate answer first. After you have worked out the answer, look back at the estimate to check that your answer makes sense.

Three plants cost £15.83, £7.36 and £24.19. What change will there be from £50?

Approximate total ➔ £16 + £7 + £24 = £47.
So the change will be approximately £3.

```
  15.83
   7.36
+ 24.19
───────
 £47.38    £50 – £47.38 = £2.62
```

Key words　　　　estimate　approximate

Rounding decimals

1 Join each of the decimals to the nearest tenth on the number line.

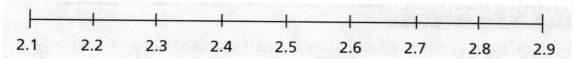

2.1   2.2   2.3   2.4   2.5   2.6   2.7   2.8   2.9

2.38   2.07   2.41   2.75   2.66   2.83

Round each of these to the nearest whole number:

2 14.063 → ☐

3 9.602 → ☐

4 23.009 → ☐

5 18.518 → ☐

6 27.905 → ☐

 6

Approximate answers

1 Can you circle the two numbers which, when multiplied together, have the answer closest to 60?

7.3   9.3   10.4   6.5

2 Circle the best estimate of 84.34 ÷ 11.86.

5   6   7   8   9   10   11

3 What is the approximate total of 3 jugs, each holding 5.485 litres? Write your answer to the nearest tenth of a litre.   _____

4 Four items from a market stall cost £2.58, £1.94, 78p and £4.03. What will be the approximate change from £10? Write your answer to the nearest 10p.   _____

5 True or false? 3.018 + 3.81 gives a greater total than 3.801 + 3.18.   _____

6 Spot the odd one out. Which of these answers is not approximately 55 to the nearest whole number? Cross out the odd one and write the number it rounds to.

13.68 + 41.41   97.38 − 42.19   11.78 × 5.19   109.89 ÷ 2

_____

6

TOTAL MARKS ☐ 12

Addition and subtraction

Adding decimals

When you have numbers to add, look to see if you can add them mentally. If they are large decimals, use a written method if you are not able to use a calculator.

When you add decimals, remember to line up the decimal points.

What is the total of 14.9, 7.24 and 0.85?

An approximate answer is 15 + 7 + 1 = 23.

Top Tip *Put zeros in to even up the number of decimal places.*

1 Write them in a column, lining up the decimal points. Start by adding from the right-hand column.

```
   14.90
    7.24
 +  0.85
 _____
       9
```

2 Keep going left until all the columns have been added.

```
   14.90
    7.24
 +  0.85
 _____
   22.99
    1 1
```

```
 14.90
  7.24
+0.85
```

Subtracting decimals

Check to see if you can work it out mentally before trying a written method.

9.4 – 3.76   An approximate answer is 9 – 4 = 5.

1 Write them in a column, lining up the decimal points. Start from the right-hand column and take away the bottom **digit** from the top digit.

```
   9.³4¹0
 – 3. 7 6
 _____
        4
```

If needed, remember to exchange a hundredth from the tenths column, renaming the numbers.

2 Now do the same with the other columns. Write it nice and clearly, so you can see the exchange and renaming of numbers.

```
   ⁸9 . ¹³4¹0
 – 3 . 7 6
 _____
   5 . 6 4
```

Key words   digit

Adding decimals

Write an approximate answer and then work out the exact answer.

1 412.79 + 178.16

2 Total 1.717 and 4.355.

3 Add 29.08 to 38.44.

4 What is the sum of 235.88 and 129.26?

5 What is the total of 2.845, 3.991 and 4.605?

Use the numbers in the grid to answer these.

6 Find four pairs of numbers that total 5.

_____

2.792	2.614	3.281	4.212
4.183	1.175	3.817	1.943
3.825	2.208	5.179	2.386
1.719	3.788	6.057	2.821

7 Find four pairs of numbers that total 8.

_____

7

Subtracting decimals

Look at the parcels and answer these.

A   B    C   D   E    F

A 3.245kg   **B** 11.88kg   **C** 2.915kg   **D** 4.203kg   **E** 12.79kg   **F** 16.24kg

1 What is the difference in weight between parcels **F** and **B**?   _____

2 How much more does parcel **D** weigh than parcel **A**?   _____

3 How much less does parcel **E** weigh than parcel **F**?   _____

4 Which parcel weighs 0.33kg less than parcel **A**?   _____

5 Which two parcels have a difference in weight of 0.91kg?   _____

5

TOTAL MARKS   12

Multiplication

Column method of multiplication

If the numbers are too large to multiply mentally, a column method or a grid method can be used.

This is the column method. Always estimate an approximate answer first.

What is 387 multiplied by 43? 387 × 43 is approximately 400 × 40 = 16000.

```
    387                → leading to →            387
  ×  43                                        ×  43
  ─────                                        ─────
  12000   (300 × 40)                           15480   (387 × 40)
   3200   (80 × 40)                             1161   (387 × 3)
    280   (7 × 40)                             ─────
    900   (300 × 3)                            16641
    240   (80 × 3)
     21   (7 × 3)
  ─────
  16641
```

Grid method

For this method, the numbers are **partitioned** into hundreds, tens and ones, and written around a grid. Multiply each pair of numbers to complete the grid and add up each row to find the total.

What is 387 multiplied by 43?

×	300	80	7		
40	12000	3200	280	→	15480
3	900	240	21	→	1161

Total: 16641

 This method can be used to multiply 2, 3 or 4 digit numbers. Remember to estimate an answer first.

Key words   partition

Column method of multiplication

Use the column method of multiplying to answer these.

1 438 × 17 = _____

2 392 × 23 = _____

3 286 × 34 = _____

Write the missing digit for each part of the sum.

4 2 __ 3 × 34 = 860 __

5 __15 × 29 = 1203 __

6 517 × __ 2 = 1654 __

6

Grid method

Use the grid method of multiplying to answer these.

1 294 × 18 = [ ]

2 367 × 24 = [ ]

3 293 × 35 = [ ]

Choose your preferred method to answer these.

4 There are 125 computer discs in a box. How many computer discs are there in 38 boxes?

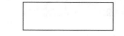

5 Daniel travels a total of 37.8km going to and from work each day. How far does he travel in five days?

6 A garden is 29 metres long and 9.8 metres wide. What is the area of the garden?

7 Sally saved £12.50 a week for 35 weeks. How much has she saved altogether?

8 Taking a shower uses approximately 35 litres of water. If you have a shower every day for a year, how much water would that use?

9 A small bottle of vinegar contains 455ml. An extra large bottle contains eight times as much. How many litres does the extra large bottle of vinegar hold?

9

TOTAL MARKS [ ] 15

Division

Written methods

Before you start on a written division, work out an approximate answer first.

What is 889 divided by 6?

> 889 ÷ 6 is approximately 900 ÷ 6, so it will be a little less than 150.

Remember, if a number cannot be divided exactly, it leaves a remainder.

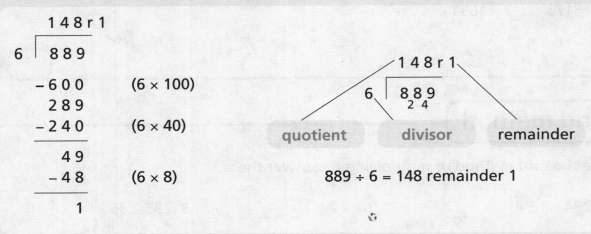

```
      1 4 8 r 1
  6 | 8 8 9
   - 6 0 0      (6 × 100)
     2 8 9
   - 2 4 0      (6 × 40)
       4 9
     - 4 8      (6 × 8)
         1
```

```
        1 4 8 r 1
  6 |   8 8 9
         2 4
```

quotient   divisor   remainder

889 ÷ 6 = 148 remainder 1

Quotients as decimals

With some division questions, particularly with money or measures, the answer is not correct with a remainder. An exact number is needed with a decimal answer. Use the short method shown above, but put a decimal point and zeros after the decimal point, so that you can continue dividing the number.

> £769 is divided amongst four people.
> How much do they each get?

```
        1 9 2 . 2 5
  4 |   7 6 9 . 0 0
         3     1 2
```

How many fours in 7 hundreds?   1 hundred, with 3 hundreds remaining.

How many fours in 36 tens?   9 tens.

How many fours in 9?   2, with 1 remaining.

How many fours in 10 tenths?   2 tenths, with 2 tenths remaining.

How many fours in 20 hundredths?   5 hundredths.

 Key words   remainder   quotient   divisor

Written methods

Answer these problems.

1   A reel of electric cable is 500m in length. It is cut into 9m
    lengths. How many complete 9m lengths will there be?

2   A floor is 324cm long and floor tiles are 8cm in length.
    How many tiles will be needed to cover one whole
    length of the wall?

3   A schoolbook has 376 pages. There are six pages in each chapter.
    How many pages are left over for the contents and answers?

4   Seven beans are planted in a row. There are 162 beans in
    a packet. How many full rows can be planted from this
    packet of beans?

5   A farmer collects 249 eggs and puts them into egg boxes
    that hold 6 eggs. All the eggs must be in an egg box.
    How many egg boxes will he need?

Top Tip Look carefully at the question to
see if the remainder needs to
round up or down for the answer.

5

Quotients as decimals

1   This piece of wood is divided into 4 equal lengths. How long is each length?

173cm

_____

2   A group of 5 people win a prize of £2342 and share it equally
    between themselves. How much do they each get?   _____

3   A water tank holds 182 litres. It is emptied and exactly fills 8
    large containers. What is the capacity of each container?   _____

4   David saves the same amount each week. After 12 weeks he
    has saved £81. How much does he save each week?   _____

5   A lorry holds 1293kg of grain. It is divided equally into
    5 containers. How much grain is in each container?   _____

5

TOTAL MARKS 10

Fractions of quantities

Fractions and division

Finding fractions of quantities is very similar to dividing amounts.

Look at these examples. What is:

$\frac{1}{3}$ of 21?

$\frac{1}{10}$ of 30?

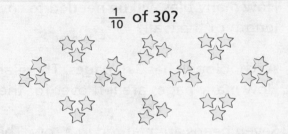

These both have 1 as a **numerator**, so simply divide by the **denominator**.

$\frac{1}{3}$ of 21 is $21 \div 3 = 7$ $\frac{1}{10}$ of 30 is $30 \div 10 = 3$

Numerator greater than 1

$\frac{1}{8}$ of 40 = 5.

This is easy because we just divide by the denominator: $40 \div 8 = 5$.

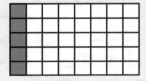

$\frac{5}{8}$ of 40 = 25

Now the numerator is 5, it means we count five of the groups.

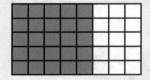

If the numerator is more than 1, divide by the denominator and then multiply by the numerator.

Look at these examples.

$\frac{2}{3}$ of 18 is $18 \div 3 = 6$, then $\times 2 = 12$

$\frac{3}{5}$ of 80 is $80 \div 5 = 16$, then $\times 3 = 48$

$\frac{7}{10}$ of 90 is $90 \div 10 = 9$, then $\times 7 = 63$

numerator?
denominator?

Top Tip *Try to work these out mentally, jotting down the division to keep a record for each part of the calculation.*

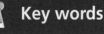 **Key words**   numerator   denominator

Fractions and division

1   Mr Adams has a total of 96 farm animals. Write the number of each farm animal owned by Mr Adams.

$\frac{1}{2}$ are chickens [ ]

$\frac{1}{4}$ are goats [ ]

$\frac{1}{6}$ are cows [ ]

$\frac{1}{12}$ are ducks [ ]

Answer these.

2 What fraction of £1 is:	3 What fraction of £2 is:	4 What fraction of £10 is:
50p _____	20p _____	£2.50 _____
20p _____	£1 _____	£5 _____
10p _____	50p _____	£1 _____
25p _____	£1.50 _____	£7.50 _____
75p _____	40p _____	£2 _____

4

Numerator greater than 1

Write < or > between each pair of amounts.

1   $\frac{5}{8}$ of 32 [ ] $\frac{3}{4}$ of 32   3 $\frac{3}{4}$ of 48 [ ] $\frac{5}{6}$ of 48

2   $\frac{2}{3}$ of 60 [ ] $\frac{3}{5}$ of 60   4 $\frac{6}{7}$ of 28 [ ] $\frac{3}{4}$ of 28

Join the matching questions and answers.

5 190	6 342	7 268	8 291	9 301

$\frac{2}{3}$ of 402	$\frac{3}{4}$ of 456	$\frac{3}{5}$ of 485	$\frac{5}{8}$ of 304	$\frac{7}{10}$ of 430

9

TOTAL MARKS [ ] 13

29

Percentages of quantities

Percentages of a quantity

What is 20% of £320?

There are several methods you could use to solve this type of percentage question.

Method 1
Change to a fraction and work it out:

$20\% = \frac{20}{100} = \frac{1}{5}$

$\frac{1}{5}$ of £320 = £320 ÷ 5 = £64

Method 2
Use 10% to work it out – just divide the number by 10:

10% of £320 is £32. So, 20% of £32 is double that: £64.

Method 3
If you are allowed, use a calculator to work it out:

Key in:

20 ÷ 100 × 320 =

 Top Tip To find 5%, remember that it is half of 10%.

 TV only £320

Percentage decreases and increases

Discounts and sales often have percentage decreases.

A car costing £5600 has a 10% discount. What is the sale price?

Step 1
Work out the percentage:

10% of £5600 is £560.

Step 2
Take away this amount from the price:

£5600 – £560 = £5040

So the sale price of the car is £5040.

For a percentage increase, there are still two steps, but you add the percentage to the price.

A bottle normally has 920ml of sauce, but this is increased by 5%. How much sauce is now in the bottle?

Step 1
Work out the percentage:

5% of 920ml is 46ml.

Step 2
Add this to the original amount:

920 + 46 is 966
So the new amount is 966ml.

 Key words   percentage

Answers

PAGE 5
Answering problems
1. £60
2. 12.35kg
3. 21
4. 10

Multi-step problems
1. £264.10
2. Bag of 12 rolls: £2.24
   Offer: Buy 1 bag, get 1 bag half price
3. 212g
4. £19.12

PAGE 7
Reasoning
1. 6
2. 78
3. 276
4. 70p
5. True. Add the largest 3-digit number.
   999 + 999 = 1998

Finding all possibilities
1. 47 and 48
2. X = 1225   Y = 775
3. 7 black beads
4. 6.2cm and 8.4cm or 7.3cm and 7.3cm
5. $3 \times 7 \times 11$

PAGE 9
Number sequences
1. Rule: + 5   Yes
2. Rule: + 3   No
3. Rule: – 6   No
4. Rule: – 4   Yes
5. Rule: + 30   No

Formulae and equations
1. $h = 8$
2. $y = 4$
3. $r = 7$
4. $4n – 2$
5. 15

PAGE 11
Ordering decimals
1. 9.841
2. 1.489
3. 8.941
4. 1.849 or 1.894
5. 1.489, 1.849 or 1.894, 8.941, 9.841

Negative numbers
1. 12°
2. 23°
3. 11°
4. 7 and –11
5. –11°C, –8°C, –4°C, 1.5°C, 6°C, 8.5°C

PAGE 13
Equivalent fractions
1. $\frac{3}{4}$
2. $\frac{3}{5}$
3. $\frac{3}{4}$
4. $\frac{1}{3}$
5. $\frac{2}{5}$

Comparing fractions
1. Any one of these fractions: $\frac{7}{8}, \frac{5}{8}, \frac{2}{3}, \frac{3}{5}, \frac{5}{7}$
2. Many possibilities. Check answer.
3. $\frac{4}{5}$ is larger because $\frac{2}{3} = \frac{10}{15}$ and $\frac{4}{5} = \frac{12}{15}$
4. Many possibilities. Check answer.
   E.g. $\frac{5}{16}$
5. Many possibilities. Check answer.
   E.g. $\frac{8}{15}, \frac{7}{15}, \frac{2}{5}$

PAGE 15
Percentages and fractions
1. 70%
2. 80%
3. 76%
4. 80%

Equivalent values
1. $\frac{1}{2} = 0.5 = 50\%$
2. $\frac{1}{4} = 0.25 = 25\%$
3. $\frac{1}{20} = 0.05 = 5\%$
4. $\frac{2}{5} = 0.4 = 40\%$
5. $\frac{17}{50} = 0.34 = 34\%$
6. $\frac{7}{10} = 0.7 = 70\%$
7. $\frac{9}{100} = 0.09 = 9\%$
8. $\frac{11}{25} = 0.44 = 44\%$
9. $25\% = 0.25$
10. $0.2 = 20\%$
11. $0.75 > 57\%$
12. $4\% < 0.4$
13. $8\% < 0.8$
14. $0.1 = 10\%$
15. $7\% = 0.07$
16. $\frac{2}{5} = 0.4$

PAGE 17
Ratio
1. 6
2. 15
3. 16 litres
4. 1 carton of cranberry juice
5. 4:1

Direct proportion
1. butter ➜ 150g, flour ➜ 200g, grated carrots ➜ 100g, sugar ➜ 60g, beaten eggs ➜ 50g, walnuts ➜ 40g
2. 225g
3. 7.5cm
4. £7.50
5. 0.06l or 60ml

PAGE 19
Factors
1. 1, 2, 3, <u>6</u>
2. 1, 3, 5, <u>15</u>
3. 1, 2, 7, <u>14</u>
4. 1, 2, 3, <u>6</u>
5. 1, 2, 3, <u>6</u>

Multiples
1. 2 and 4
2. 3 and 9
3. 2, 4 and 5
4. 2, 3, 4 and 6
5. 2, 3, 4, 6 and 9
6. 2, 3, 4, 5, 6 and 9
7. 36

Prime factors
1. $7 \times 3 \times 4$
2. $3 \times 4 \times 11$
3. $5 \times 11 \times 13$

PAGE 21
Rounding decimals
1.

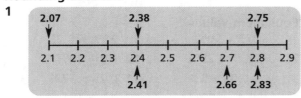

2. 14
3. 10
4. 23
5. 19
6. 28

Approximate answers
1. 9.3 and 6.5
2. 7
3. 16.5 litres
4. 70p
5. False
6. 11.78×5.19 Rounds to 61.

PAGE 23
Adding decimals
1. approx: 591,   590.95
2. approx: 6.1,   6.072
3. approx: 67 or 67.5,   67.52
4. approx: 365,   365.14
5. approx: 11.4 or 11.45,   11.441
6. 2.614 + 2.386, 2.792 + 2.208, 3.281 + 1.719, 3.825 + 1.175
7. 3.788 + 4.212, 5.179 + 2.821, 4.183 + 3.817, 6.057 + 1.943

Subtracting decimals
1. 4.36kg
2. 0.958kg
3. 3.45kg
4. C
5. B and E

PAGE 25
Column method of multiplication
1. 7446
2. 9016
3. 9724
4. $253 \times 34 = 8602$
5. $415 \times 29 = 12035$
6. $517 \times 32 = 16544$

Grid method
1. 5292
2. 8808
3. 10255
4. 4750
5. 189km
6. $284.2m^2$
7. £437.50
8. 12775 litres
9. 3.64l

PAGE 27
Written methods
1. 55 lengths
2. 41 tiles
3. 4 pages
4. 23 rows
5. 42 boxes

Quotients as decimals
1. 43.25cm
2. £468.40
3. 22.75 litres
4. £6.75
5. 258.6kg

PAGE 29
Fractions and division
1. 48 chickens, 24 goats, 16 cows, 8 ducks
2. 50p ➜ $\frac{1}{2}$, 20p ➜ $\frac{1}{5}$, 10p ➜ $\frac{1}{10}$, 25p ➜ $\frac{1}{4}$, 75p ➜ $\frac{3}{4}$
3. 20p ➜ $\frac{1}{10}$, £1 ➜ $\frac{1}{2}$, 50p ➜ $\frac{1}{4}$, £1.50 ➜ $\frac{3}{4}$, 40p ➜ $\frac{1}{5}$
4. £2.50 ➜ $\frac{1}{4}$, £5 ➜ $\frac{1}{2}$, £1 ➜ $\frac{1}{10}$, £7.50 ➜ $\frac{3}{4}$, £2 ➜ $\frac{1}{5}$

Numerator greater than 1

1 $\frac{5}{8}$ of 32 < $\frac{3}{4}$ of 32
2 $\frac{2}{3}$ of 60 > $\frac{3}{5}$ of 60
3 $\frac{3}{4}$ of 48 < $\frac{5}{6}$ of 48
4 $\frac{6}{7}$ of 28 > $\frac{3}{4}$ of 28
5 190 = $\frac{5}{8}$ of 304
6 342 = $\frac{3}{4}$ of 456
7 268 = $\frac{2}{3}$ of 402
8 291 = $\frac{3}{5}$ of 485
9 301 = $\frac{7}{10}$ of 430

PAGE 31
Percentages of a quantity

1 £5, £15
2 £8, £32
3 £2.50, £7.50
4 £20, £2
5 £4, £2
6 £27, £54
7 £60, £720
8 £9, £27

Percentage decreases and increases

1 280
2 225 litres
3 672 chairs
4 £3420
5 540g
6 650ml
7 276 pages

PAGE 33
Using a calculator

1 51.8
2 18.2
3 79.5
4 511m²
5 102.2m²

Squares and square roots

1 1892.25cm²
2 27cm
3 18
4 37
5 8.4

Using brackets

1 206.55
2 533.544
3 22.95
4 32.3
5 13.16

PAGE 35
Triangles

1 sometimes
2 never
3 sometimes
4 never
5 sometimes
6 always

Quadrilaterals

1

☑ ☐ ☑ ☐ ☑ ☑

2

	quadrilateral	not a quadrilateral
1 or more lines of symmetry	A C D	F G
no lines of symmetry	E H	B

PAGE 37
Parts of 3D shapes

1 2 triangular faces and 3 rectangular faces.
2 6 square faces.
3 4 triangular faces.
4 2 hexagonal faces and 6 rectangular faces.
5 1 square face and 4 triangular faces.
6 4 rectangular faces and 2 square faces.

Nets of solids

1 square-based pyramid
2 triangular prism
3 cuboid
4 tetrahedron
5 hexagonal prism
6 cube

PAGE 39
Moving shapes

1 rotated
2 reflected
3 translated
4 reflected
5 Check pattern.

Rotational symmetry

		Number of lines of symmetry				
		0	1	2	3	4
Order of rotational symmetry	1		D			
	2	B				
	3	E			C	
	4					A

PAGE 41
Positions on a grid

1 Check accuracy.
2 (3,−5) (5,−3) (5,1) (3,1)

Shapes and coodinates

1 (48,20)
2 (75,40)

PAGE 43
Measuring angles

1 79°
2 83°
3 160°
4 Check accuracy.
5 a = 35° b = 93°

Angles and shapes

1 x = 30°
2 p = 67°, q = 67°, r = 23°

Angles and lines

1 142°
2 85°
3 a = 65°, b = 115°, c = 65°
4 p = 131°, q = 49°, r = 131°
5 144°

PAGE 45
Units of measure
1	28 cupfuls	5	3.4kg
2	50 bags	6	29kg
3	30 days	7	1.4 litres
4	3 laps		

Imperial measures
1	1.8m	3	10km
2	9 pints	4	4kg

PAGE 47
Area of rectangles
1	62.56m^2	2	151.2m^2

Area of right-angled triangles
1 Check area is 8 squares.
2 Check area is 15 squares.
3 Check area is 12 squares.

Composite shapes
1

2 217cm^2
3 142.76m^2

PAGE 49
The probability scale
1 $\frac{1}{2}$ or evens
2 Check answer – either certain or impossible, depending on the day today.
3 impossible or 0
4 $\frac{1}{2}$ or evens
5 certain

Equally likely outcomes
1 a $\frac{1}{6}$ d 0
   b $\frac{1}{2}$ e 1
   c $\frac{1}{3}$
2 A → 1 in 6 chance, B → 1 in 8 chance
3 Both have a 1 in 2 chance.

PAGE 51
Frequency charts and grouped data
Answers 1–3 are approximate.
1 43
2 97
3 26
4 Not enough information to say.
5 This is true.

Time/distance graphs
1 9.30
2 40km
3 10.00
4 0km (it did not move)
5 48km/h

PAGE 53
Mode
1	24	3	32kg
2	9.2cm	4	106

Median
1	34	3	322g
2	230	4	7m

Mean
1	34	4	520ml
2	0.6	5	8.4km
3	6.25cm		

PAGE 55
Interpreting pie charts
1	interlocking plastic bricks	3	2
		4	50%
2	$\frac{1}{6}$	5	wooden bricks

Comparing pie charts
1	20%	4	False
2	$\frac{3}{8}$	5	Ali
3	£10		

Letts Educational
4 Grosvenor Place, London SW1X 7DL
School enquiries: 015395 64911/65921
Parent & student enquiries: 015395 64913
E-mail: mail@lettsandlonsdale.co.uk

Website: www.letts-educational.com

First published 2008

Editorial and design: 2ibooks [publishing solutions] Cambridge

Author: Paul Broadbent
Book concept and development: Helen Jacobs, Publishing Director
Editorial: Sophie London, Senior Commissioning Editor
       Katy Knight, Editorial Assistant
Illustrators: Andy Roberts and Phillip Burrows
Cover design: Angela English

British Library Cataloging in Publication Data. A CIP record of this book is available from the British Library.

ISBN 9781843158820

Text, design and illustration © Letts Educational Limited 2008

Printed in Italy

Percentages of a quantity

Write the percentages of each of these amounts.

1 £50

10% ➔ £ ☐

30% ➔ £ ☐

2 £80

10% ➔ £ ☐

40% ➔ £ ☐

3 £25

10% ➔ £ ☐

30% ➔ £ ☐

4 £200

10% ➔ £ ☐

1% ➔ £ ☐

5 £40

10% ➔ £ ☐

5% ➔ £ ☐

6 £2700

1% ➔ £ ☐

2% ➔ £ ☐

7 £6000

1% ➔ £ ☐

12% ➔ £ ☐

8 £180

5% ➔ £ ☐

15% ➔ £ ☐

8

Percentage decreases and increases

1 Last year there were 350 scouts at a scout parade. This year there were 20% fewer scouts. How many scouts were there in total this year? ☐

2 A barrel of oil holds 300 litres when full. 25% of the oil is used up. How many litres of oil are still in the barrel? ☐

3 960 chairs are put in a hall for a show on Tuesday night. 30% fewer chairs are needed the following night. How many chairs are needed in total on the Wednesday night? ☐

4 A car is being sold for £3600. The car dealer decides to reduce the price by 5%. What is its new price? ☐

Write the new amounts for each of these.

5

New box: ☐ g

6

New bottle: ☐ ml

7

New total of pages: ☐

7

Calculators

Using a calculator

Make sure you know how to use these keys on a calculator.

+/− changes a positive number to a negative number

C or CE clears the last entry – useful if you make a mistake halfway through a sum.

% percentage, e.g. to find 40% of £60, key in
6 0 × 4 0 % is £24. Don't press = .

√ square root (inverse of a square number), e.g. to find the square root of 144, press 1 4 4 then the √ key.

AC clears all entries and leaves 0 .

Squares and square roots

Numbers multiplied by themselves make square numbers: $3 \times 3 = 9$. A short way of writing 3×3 is 3^2, which is 3 squared.

Square roots (√) are the opposite to square numbers. To find the square root of 25, find which number, when multiplied by itself, makes 25. So $\sqrt{25} = 5$. The square root key on calculators is useful for finding square roots that are not whole numbers. For example, we know the square root of 90 will be between 9 ($\sqrt{81}$) and 10 ($\sqrt{100}$). The calculator gives the actual number: 9.487.

Using brackets

When part of a problem is in brackets, you work out the bracket part first.

15 − (8 + 4)   (15 − 8) + 4

15 − 12 = 3   7 + 4 = 11

Top Tip *Many calculators have different keys, so get used to the one you have and practise different calculations.*

Calculators will ignore brackets unless you have a calculator with a bracket key, so make sure you key this part of the calculation first and write it down or put it into the calculator memory. Try the calculations above on your calculator.

Key words   square number   square root

Using a calculator

Use a calculator to work out the missing numbers.

1 445.48 ÷ ☐ = 8.6

3 30528 ÷ ☐ = 384

2 34.7 × ☐ = 631.54

Here is a plan of a garden.

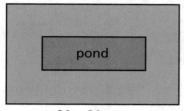

pond

17m 50cm

29m 20cm

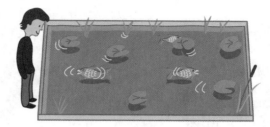

4 What is the area of the whole garden, including the pond? ☐ m²

5 The pond takes up 20% of the garden.
What is the area of the pond? ☐ m²

5

Squares and square roots

1 Each side of a square is 435mm.
What is the area of the square in square centimetres? ☐

2 A square has an area of 729cm². What is the length of each side? ☐ cm

3 Calculate the square root of each of these.

√324 ☐   **4** √1369 ☐   **5** √70.56 ☐

5

Using brackets

Answer these.

1 250 – (27.79 + 15.66) = ☐

4 35.9 – (18 × 0.2) = ☐

2 51.6 × (3.44 + 6.9) = ☐

5 0.7 × (38.6 – 19.8) = ☐

3 (14.5 × 3.5) – (8.1 + 19.7) = ☐

5

TOTAL MARKS ☐ 15

2D shapes

Triangles

Look at the properties of these different triangles:

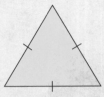 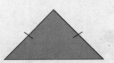 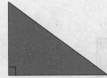 

Equilateral

3 equal sides.
3 equal angles of
60°. 3 lines of
symmetry.

Isosceles

2 equal sides.
2 equal angles.
1 line of
symmetry.

Right-angled

One angle is a
right angle, 90°.

Scalene

No equal sides.
No equal angles.

Quadrilaterals

These are some special four-sided shapes. Look carefully at their properties to
sort out similarities and differences.

Square

4 equal sides.
4 equal angles of 90°.
Opposite sides **parallel**.
4 lines of symmetry.

Rectangle

2 pairs of equal sides.
4 equal angles of 90°.
Opposite sides parallel.
2 lines of symmetry.

Rhombus

4 equal sides.
Opposite angles equal.
Opposite sides parallel.

Parallelogram

Opposite sides are
equal and parallel.

Kite

Two pairs of **adjacent**
sides are equal.

Trapezium

One pair of parallel
sides.

 *Some shapes have no lines of symmetry and others have more than one line of
symmetry. Try to picture the 'fold lines' on a shape that would fold it exactly
in half and count the number of different ways it can be folded in half.*

 Key words   symmetry   parallel   adjacent

Triangles

Circle *always*, *sometimes* or *never* for each of these statements.

1   A triangle has 3 acute angles.   always   sometimes   never

2   A triangle has 2 obtuse angles.   always   sometimes   never

3   A triangle has 2 perpendicular sides.   always   sometimes   never

4   A triangle has 2 parallel sides.   always   sometimes   never

5   An isosceles triangle has an obtuse angle.   always   sometimes   never

6   An equilateral triangle has 3 lines of symmetry.   always   sometimes   never

6

Quadrilaterals

1   Laura's dictionary gives this definition for a parallelogram:
    'A parallelogram is a quadrilateral that has two pairs of parallel sides.'
    Using this definition, tick each parallelogram for one mark each:

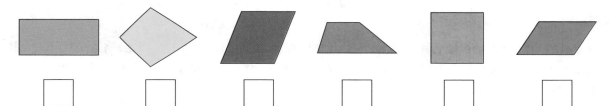

☐   ☐   ☐   ☐   ☐   ☐

2   Write the letter which represents each of these shapes in the correct part of
    this Carroll diagram.

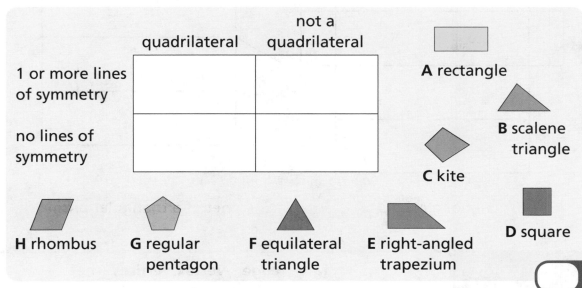

14

TOTAL MARKS ⬭ 20

3D shapes

Parts of 3D shapes

3D shapes are made up of **faces**, **edges** and **vertices** (or corners).

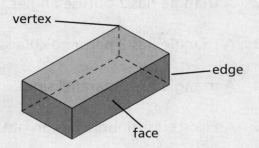

A face is a surface of a solid.

An edge is where two faces meet.

A vertex is where three or more edges meet.

A cuboid has 6 faces, 12 edges and 8 vertices.

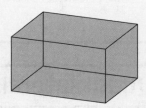

There is a relationship between the number of faces, edges and vertices of shapes. Euler wrote it as a formula:
Number of Faces + Number of Vertices – Number of Edges = 2
Test the formula F + V – N = 2 on different 3D shapes.

Nets of solids

The **net** of a shape is what it looks like when it is opened out flat. Carefully pull open a cereal box so that it is one large piece of cardboard – this is the net of the box.

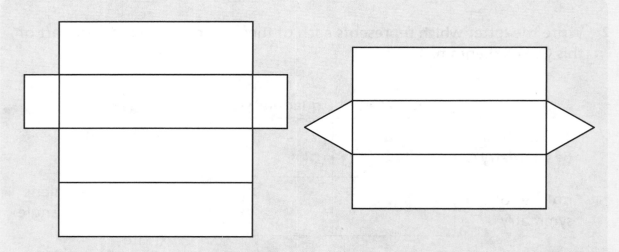

net of a cuboid   net of a triangular prism

 Key words   **face   edge   vertex/vertices   net**

Parts of 3D shapes

Match each description to the shape it describes to complete the sentence.

1	A triangular prism has …	4 triangular faces.
2	A cube has …	2 hexagonal faces and 6 rectangular faces.
3	A tetrahedron has …	2 triangular faces and 3 rectangular faces.
4	A hexagonal prism has …	4 rectangular faces and 2 square faces.
5	A square-based pyramid has …	6 square faces.
6	A cuboid has …	1 square face and 4 triangular faces.

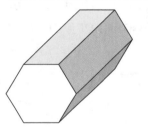

6

Nets of solids

Write the name of each of these shapes from its net.

1 _____

4 _____

2 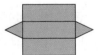 _____

5  _____

3 _____

6 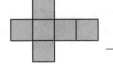 _____

6

TOTAL MARKS   12

Movement geometry

Moving shapes

A shape can be moved by:

Rotation: a shape can be rotated about a point, clockwise or anticlockwise.

Shape A is rotated 180° around point X.

Reflection: this is sometimes called flipping over.

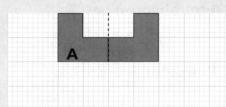

Shape A is reflected. The dotted line is a line of reflection.

Translation: this is sliding a shape across, up, down or diagonally, without rotating or flipping over.

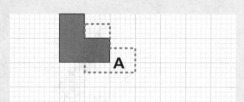

Shape A has moved 5 squares across and 2 squares down.

Rotational symmetry

If you can turn or rotate a shape and fit it onto itself in a different position to the original, then it has rotational **symmetry**. The red dots show the centre of rotation.

The order of rotational symmetry is the number of times the shape can turn to fit onto itself until it comes back to the original position.
Every shape has an order of rotational symmetry of at least 1, so just count the shapes with an order of 2, 3, 4 or more.

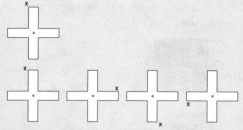

This cross has an order of rotational symmetry of 4.

 Key words   clockwise   anticlockwise   symmetry

Moving shapes

Write whether these shapes have been translated, rotated or reflected.

1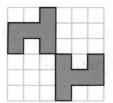

2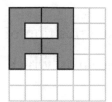

3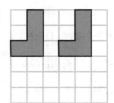

_____   _____   _____

This tile is used to make a pattern.

4 Has this tile been rotated, translated or reflected to make this pattern?

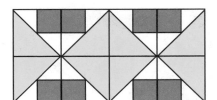

5 Use the tile to draw a different pattern. Is it a translation, rotation or reflection?

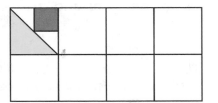

_____

_____

5

Rotational symmetry

A square has 4 lines of symmetry and it has an order of rotational symmetry of 4. The letter A is written on the grid below to show this. Write the letter of each shape in the correct space on the grid.

		Number of lines of symmetry				
		0	1	2	3	4
Order of rotational symmetry	1					
	2					
	3					
	4					A

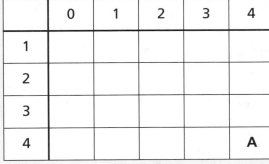

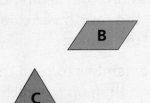

Top Tip *Use a mirror to check lines of symmetry, and tracing paper to work out the order of rotational symmetry of shapes.*

4

Coordinates

Positions on a grid

Coordinates are used to show the exact position of a point on a grid.

Two numbers from the x **axis** and the y axis, which could include negative numbers, show the position.

The coordinates of A are (–4,1).

The coordinates of B are (1,2).

The coordinates of C are (4,–3).

Coordinates are always written in brackets and separated by a comma.

This grid has 4 **quadrants**, with negative numbers on the x axis and the y axis.

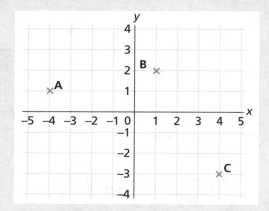

 Top Tip *The numbers on the horizontal x axis are written first, then the vertical y axis. You can remember this because x comes before y and x is a cross!*

Shapes and coordinates

Coordinates are very useful for plotting the vertices of shapes.

Here are two sides of a square.

- What are the coordinates of the three vertices?

- Mark the missing coordinates for the fourth vertex and complete the square.

Remember to read the numbers across and then up for each position.

Draw in the missing lines, using a ruler to make it as accurate as possible.

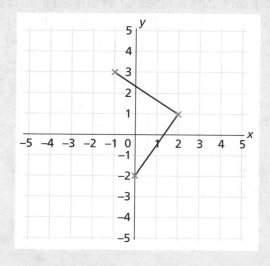

 Key words   axis   horizontal   vertical   quadrant

Positions on a grid

Translate this shape so that it is 4 squares across to the right and 2 squares down.
Draw the new shape.

1

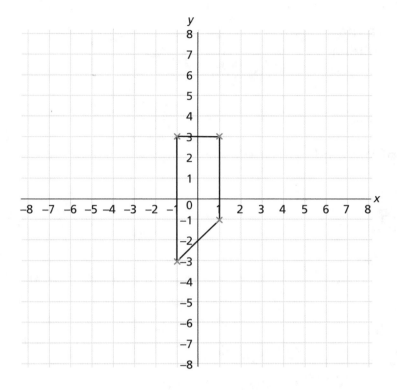

What are the coordinates of the vertices of your translated shape?

2 (☐ , ☐), (☐ , ☐),(☐ , ☐),(☐ , ☐)

☐ 2

Shapes and coordinates

1 This is an isosceles triangle.
What is the missing coordinate?

(☐ , ☐)

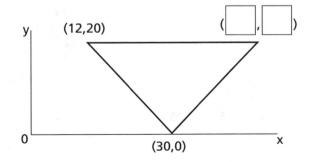

2 This is a rectangle. What is
the missing coordinate?

(☐ , ☐)

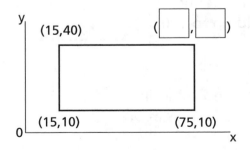

☐ 2

TOTAL MARKS ☐ 4

Lines and angles

Measuring angles

A **protractor** is used to measure the degree of an angle. It is a good idea to estimate the angle first and then measure it.

Read from the 0° on the outer scale.

Place the cross at the point of the angle you are measuring.

This angle is 45°.

Angles and shapes

All the angles of a triangle add up to 180°.

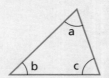

$a + b + c = 180°$

All the angles of a quadrilateral add up to 360°.

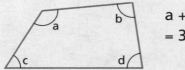

$a + b + c + d = 360°$

To find the value of missing angles on a triangle, find the total of the angles given and take it away from 180°.

$35° + 90° = 125°$
$180° - 125° = 55°$
The missing angle is 55°.

Angles and lines

Angles on a straight line add up to 180°.

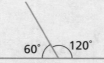

Angles at a point add up to 360°.

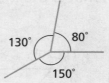

Perpendicular lines meet or cross at 90°.

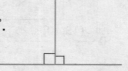

When two lines cross, the opposite angles are equal.

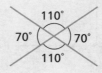

Key words   protractor   perpendicular

Measuring angles

One angle of this quadrilateral is 38°.
Measure the other three angles
accurately using a protractor.

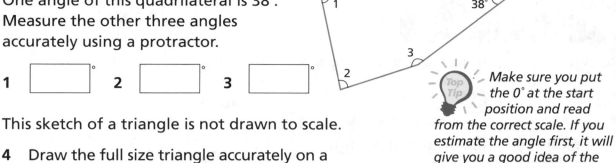

1 [   ]°   **2** [   ]°   **3** [   ]°

This sketch of a triangle is not drawn to scale.

4 Draw the full size triangle accurately on a
piece of paper. Use a protractor and a ruler.

5 Measure the size of the other two angles.

a = [   ]°   b = [   ]°

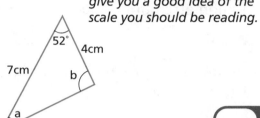

> **Top Tip** *Make sure you put
> the 0° at the start
> position and read
> from the correct scale. If you
> estimate the angle first, it will
> give you a good idea of the
> scale you should be reading.*

[5]

Angles and shapes

Do not use a protractor for these questions.

1 Calculate the size of angle x on this isosceles triangle. [   ]°

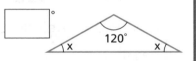

2 Rectangle ABCD has a diagonal line AD.
Calculate the size of angles p, q and r.

p = [   ]°   q = [   ]°   r = [   ]°

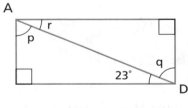

[2]

Angles and lines

Calculate the missing angles. Do not use a protractor.

1 [   ]°

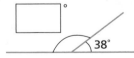

38°

2 [   ]°

95°

3

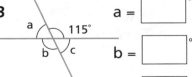

a   115°
b   c

a = [   ]°

b = [   ]°

c = [   ]°

4

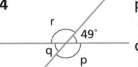

r
49°
q
p

p = [   ]°

q = [   ]°

r = [   ]°

5

145°
71°

[   ]°

[5]

Measures

Units of measure

Length, weight (or mass) and capacity are all measured using different units.

Length

1 centimetre (cm) = 10 millimetres (mm)
1 metre (m) = 100 centimetres (cm)
1 kilometre (km) = 1000 metres (m)

Weight

1 kilogram (kg) = 1000 grams (g)
1 tonne = 1000kg

Capacity

1 litre (l) = 1000 millilitres (ml)
1 centilitre (cl) = 100ml

It is important to write the units in your answers and remember that different units can be used for **equivalent** amounts.

This mirror is 1.825m or 1825mm high.

This bottle holds 2.855 litres or 2855 millilitres.

This feather weighs 0.064kg or 64g.

Imperial measures

We still sometimes use imperial units, which are measures that were used in the past. Try to learn these approximate metric values:

Length	Weight	Capacity
12 inches = 1 foot	16 ounces = 1 pound (lb)	8 pints = 1 gallon
2.5cm ≈ 1 inch	25g ≈ 1 ounce	1.75 pints ≈ 1 litre
30cm ≈ 1 foot	2.25lb ≈ 1kg	4.5 litres ≈ 1 gallon
3 feet ≈ 1 metre		
5 miles ≈ 8km		

Top Tip

Remember that ≈ means "is approximately equal to".

Key words   equivalent

Units of measure

1 A jug holds 3.5 litres of fruit juice. How many 125ml cupfuls will this fill?

2 There is 40g of sauce in 1 bag. How many bags are there in a 2kg pack?

3 A packet contains 2.7kg of rabbit food. Sam feeds his rabbit with 90g of feed each day. How many days does the packet of feed last?

4 During an athletics training session, Jenny runs 12 laps of a 400-metre track. She wants to run a total of 6km. How many more laps does she need to run?

Write the amounts shown for each of these.

5

6

7

 PRACTISE MEASURING

7

Imperial measures

Underline the best answers for each of these.

1 A man is 6 feet tall. Approximately how many metres is this?

0.4m   1.2m   1.5m   1.8m   2.5m

2 Approximately how many pints are there in 5 litres?

4 pints   7 pints   9 pints   11 pints   15 pints

3 Approximately how many kilometres are there in 6 miles?

2km   5km   8km   10km   18km

4 George catches a 9-pound fish. What is the approximate weight of the fish in kilograms?

1kg   4kg   6kg   7kg   10kg

4

TOTAL MARKS   11

Area

Area of rectangles

The **area** of a shape is the amount of surface that it covers. You can often measure the area of shapes by counting squares. The area of a rectangle can be found without counting if you know the length and width.

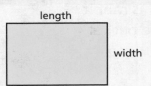

The area is length × width.

Area = 5.5cm × 3.5cm = 19.25cm^2

Top Tip *Area is usually measured in square centimetres or square metres, written as cm^2 and m^2. Always remember to write this at the end of the measurement.*

Area of right-angled triangles

Look at this right-angled triangle. It is half a rectangle.

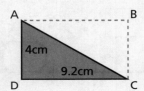

The area of the rectangle ABCD is 4cm × 9.2cm = 36.8cm^2.

The area of the right-angled triangle ACD is half the area of the rectangle ABCD.

$\frac{1}{2}$ of 36.8cm = 18.4cm^2.

The area of a right-angled triangle is: $\frac{1}{2}$ (area of the rectangle)

or

$\frac{1}{2}$ (base × height).

Composite shapes

You might be asked to find the area of a shape that is made up from different rectangles or triangles joined together. Just find the area of each part and then add them together.

Area of rectangle is 4.8cm × 2cm = 9.6cm^2.

Area of square is 2.5cm × 2.5cm = 6.25cm^2.

Total area = 15.85cm^2.

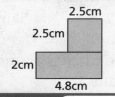

Key words area

46

Area of rectangles

Calculate the area of each of these gardens.

1

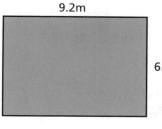

9.2m

6.8m

☐ m²

2

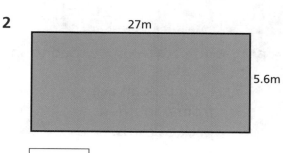

27m

5.6m

☐ m²

2

Area of right-angled triangles

On the grid, draw triangles with the same area as each coloured rectangle. Use a ruler.

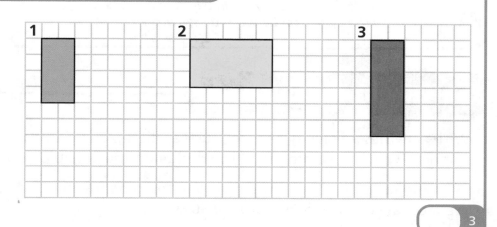

1   **2**   **3**

3

Composite shapes

1 On this grid, draw 3 more lines to make a parallelogram with an area of 12 squares.

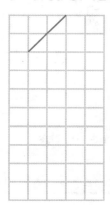

2 A star is made from this square and four triangles. What is the total area of the star?

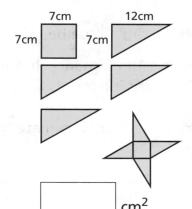

7cm   12cm

7cm   7cm

☐ cm²

3 What is the area of the garden that is grass?

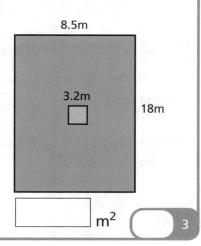

8.5m

3.2m

18m

☐ m²

3

TOTAL MARKS ☐ 8

Probability

The probability scale

A **probability scale** can be used to show how likely an event is to happen:

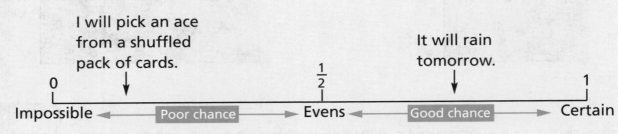

I will pick an ace from a shuffled pack of cards.

It will rain tomorrow.

0     $\frac{1}{2}$ 1

Impossible ← Poor chance → Evens ← Good chance → Certain

Top Tip

Remember: 0 is impossible – there needs to be absolutely no chance of it happening, and 1 is certain – it will absolutely, definitely happen. Most events lie somewhere in between these two extremes.

Equally likely outcomes

With activities involving 'chance', such as dice, playing cards, coin tossing or spinners, we can use probability to decide on the possible or likely outcomes.

Even chance is an equal chance of something happening as not happening. We also say a 1 in 2 chance or a 50:50 chance.

Tossing a coin – there is an even chance of it landing on heads.

Rolling a dice – there is an even chance that it will land on an odd number.

Look at this bag of beads. What is the probability of picking out a red bead?

There are 12 beads and 6 of them are red.

$\frac{6}{12}$ is the same as $\frac{1}{2}$, so there is a 1 in 2, or even, chance of picking out a red bead.

What is the probability of picking out a blue bead?

$\frac{2}{12}$ is the same as $\frac{1}{6}$, so there is a 1 in 6 chance. In theory, this means that for every 6 beads picked out, 1 would be blue.

Try this with the other coloured beads and estimate where these lie on the probability scale.

Key words   probability scale   even chance

The probability scale

Where do you think these statements will be on the probability scale?
Join each of them to a position on the scale.

1 When you roll a 1–6 dice, it will show an odd number.

2 Tomorrow will be Monday.

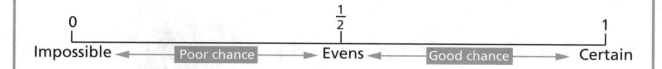

0         $\frac{1}{2}$ 1

Impossible ◄— Poor chance —► Evens ◄— Good chance —► Certain

3 A tulip will grow with no water.

4 Dropped toast will land butter side down.

5 You will have something to drink during the next week.

5

Equally likely outcomes

1 On a 1–6 dice, what is the probability of throwing…

1      $\frac{1}{3}$ $\frac{1}{2}$ $\frac{1}{6}$ 0

a a six? ☐

d a number greater than 7? ☐

b an even number? ☐

e a number between 0 and 7? ☐

c a number smaller than 3? ☐

Here are two spinners.

Spinner A   **Spinner B**

2 Why is it more likely that you would spin a 5 using Spinner **A** than Spinner **B**?

_____

3 Why are you equally likely to spin an odd number on both spinners?

_____

7

Handling data

Frequency charts and grouped data

The word frequency just means 'how many', so a frequency chart is a record of how many of something there are in a group. Frequency charts with grouped data are useful for comparing large groups of numbers.

An airport wanted to compare the weights of the luggage put onto a plane. There were over 180 bags in the survey and they all varied in weight slightly. A graph showing the individual weights would be unhelpful, so it was better to group the data to compare them.

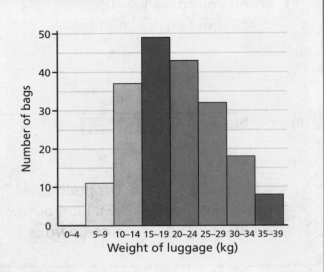

So the most common weight of luggage is between 15kg and 19kg.

Time/distance graphs

Time/distance graphs are exactly what they say – they look at the time taken for each part of a journey.

This is a record of a car journey lasting 4 hours.

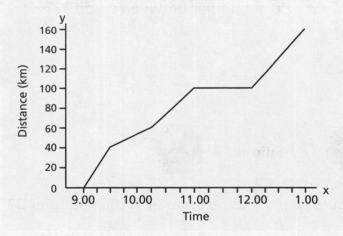

Speed is shown by kilometres per hour (km/h) or miles per hour (mph) – so this is a speed graph. The car travelled 160km in 4 hours, which is an average speed of 40km/h.

Top Tip
The steeper the line, the faster the journey – the car is travelling a greater distance over less time. The horizontal line shows that no distance was travelled for 1 hour.

Key words   frequency

Frequency charts and grouped data

Look at the grouped frequency chart on the opposite page to answer these questions.

1   How many bags weighed between 20kg and 24kg?

2   How many bags weighed less than 20kg?

3   How many bags weighed 30kg or more?

4   Read this statement: 'More bags weighed 30kg or more,
than weighed 12kg or less.' Tick one of the boxes:

This is true. ☐   This is false. ☐   Not enough information to say. ☐

5   Read this statement: 'An extra fee is paid on bags weighing 20kg or more.
Over 50% of the bags have the extra fee to pay.' Tick one of the boxes:

This is true. ☐   This is false. ☐   Not enough information to say. ☐

5

Time/distance graphs

This is a record of a coach journey.

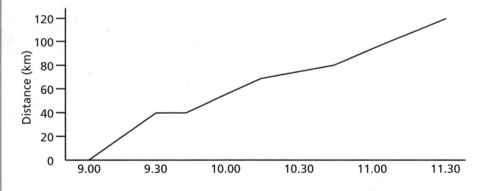

1   At what time did the coach reach its first stop? _____

2   How far did the coach travel between 9.45 and 10.45? _____

3   At approximately what time had the coach travelled 50km? _____

4   How far did the coach travel between 9.30 and 9.45? _____

5   The average speed of the journey was _____ km/h.

5

TOTAL MARKS 10

Mode, median and mean

Mode

The **mode** of a set of data is the number that occurs most often.

These are the maths test scores out of 20 for a group of children:

| 18 | 16 | 14 | 18 | 12 | 13 | 17 | 12 | 16 | 16 | 15 | 11 |

The modal average for these scores is 16 – there are more of this score than any other. So it is an average because it is more common than any other one.

Median

The **median** is the middle number in a set of numbers.

This chart shows the number of letters received each day for a week.

Monday	Tuesday	Wednesday	Thursday	Friday	Saturday	Sunday
5 letters	4 letters	8 letters	5 letters	3 letters	4 letters	1 letter

To work out the median number of letters, follow these two steps:

1 Put the numbers in order, from smallest to largest: 1, 3, 4, 4, 5, 5, 8.

2 Go to the middle number. 1, 3, 4, **4**, 5, 5, 8. So the median is 4 letters.

When working out the median for an even amount of numbers, you take the two middle numbers, add them together and divide by two.

Mean

The **mean** average is the total ÷ the number of items.

This table shows the number of bikes sold from a shop over 4 weeks.

Mean = total ÷ number of items.

9 + 14 + 18 + 23 = 64   64 ÷ 4 = 16

Week 1	Week 2	Week 3	Week 4
9	14	18	23

So the mean average number of bikes sold is 16.

 Top Tip — *The range tells us how much the information is spread. To find the range, take the smallest from the largest amount.*

 Key words   mode   median   mean

Mode

Find the mode for each of the following sets of numbers.

1 17   24   23   24   17   24   16   24   23   Mode: [   ]

2 9.2cm   8.9cm   9.5cm   8.9cm   9.2cm   9.5cm   9.2cm   Mode: [   ] cm

3 32kg   25kg   32kg   51kg   27kg   38kg   32kg   26kg   Mode: [   ] kg

4 108   108   106   101   102   106   101   106   Mode: [   ]

4

Median

Find the median for each of the following sets of numbers.

1 34   38   26   29   45   32   34   26   40   Median: [   ]

2 230   234   230   228   230   239   241   Median: [   ]

3 320g   345g   318g   344g   320g   395g   322g   Median: [   ] g

4 6.8m   7.2m   6m   8.8m   6.4m   7.2m   Median: [   ] m

 Top Tip — *Rearrange the numbers and list them in order of size to help work out any type of average.*

4

Mean

Find the mean for each of the following sets of numbers.

1 37   42   20   32   37   36   Mean: [   ]

2 0.8   0.55   0.3   0.9   0.45   Mean: [   ]

3 9cm   3cm   6cm   8cm   4cm   8cm   6cm   6cm   Mean: [   ] cm

4 300ml   250ml   700ml   450ml   900ml   Mean: [   ] ml

5 8.4km   8.2km   8.6km   8.4km   8.4km   Mean: [   ] km

5

TOTAL MARKS [   ] 13

53

Pie charts

Interpreting pie charts

Pie charts are circles divided into sections. Each section shows a number of items so that they can be compared. You could be asked to give a fraction, a percentage or a number as an answer.

A class library has 60 books. This pie chart shows the three types of books.

What fraction of the books are non-fiction?

To answer this, look at the total number of sections and the fraction of them that are non-fiction. 2 out of 5, or $\frac{2}{5}$, of the books are non-fiction books.

What percentage of the books are poetry?

$\frac{1}{5}$ of the books are poetry books. Change this to a percentage:

$\frac{1}{5} = \frac{20}{100} = 20\%$

So 20% of the books are poetry books.

How many books are fiction?

To answer each of these, you need to know what each section represents. There are 60 books altogether and the pie chart is divided into 5 parts, so each individual section represents 12 books. 2 of the sections are fiction, which means that 24 of the books are fiction books.

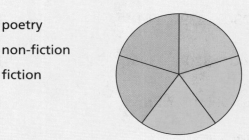

☐ poetry
☐ non-fiction
☐ fiction

Comparing pie charts

When you compare two pie charts, look carefully at the totals for each and the number of sections.

These pie charts show the results of two hockey teams. Team A played 24 matches and Team B played 18 matches.

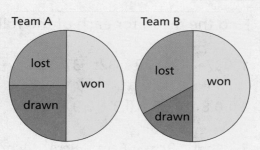

It looks like the two teams have won the same number of matches, but compare them carefully.

Team A have won $\frac{1}{2}$ of 24 matches, which is 12.

Team B have won $\frac{1}{2}$ of 18 matches, which is 9.

Key words   percentage

Interpreting pie charts

Six groups of children built towers from different materials for a problem-solving task.

This pie chart shows the materials used by the six groups to build their towers.

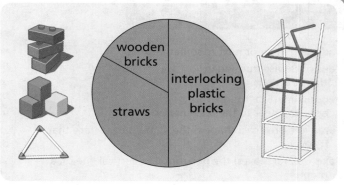

1 Which was the most popular choice of material to build a tower? _____

2 What fraction of the class used wooden bricks? _____

3 How many groups used straws? _____

4 What percentage of the class did **not** use plastic bricks? _____

5 Which type of material did only one group use? _____

5

Comparing pie charts

Tim and Ali bought some material from a DIY shop so they could each build a brick wall.

These pie charts show the material they each bought. Tim spent £140 and Ali spent £160.

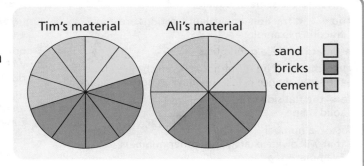

1 What percentage of his money did Tim spend on sand? _____

2 What fraction of his money did Ali spend on cement? _____

3 How much more did Tim spend on bricks than Ali? _____

4 True or false? They both spent the same proportion of their total money on sand. _____

5 Who spent the most money on cement? _____

Always look at the total for the whole 'pie' and then work out what each section is worth by seeing what fraction of the 'pie' it is.

5

TOTAL MARKS 10

55

Glossary

adjacent near or next to something

anticlockwise turning in this direction

approximate a 'rough' answer – near to the real answer

area the area of a shape is the amount of surface that it covers

axis (plural is axes) the horizontal or vertical line on a graph

clockwise turning in this direction

common denominator if two or more fractions have the same number as a denominator, then they have a common denominator

denominator the bottom number of a fraction, the number of parts it is divided into. Example: $\frac{2}{3}$

difference the difference between two numbers is the amount by which one number is greater than the other. The difference between 18 and 21 is 3

digit there are 10 digits: 0 1 2 3 4 5 6 7 8 and 9 that make all the numbers we use

divisor a divisor is a number that another number is divided by. For 32 ÷ 4 = 8, the divisor is 4

edge where two faces of a solid shape meet

equation where symbols or letters are used instead of numbers. Example: 3y = 12, so y = 4

equivalent two numbers or measures are equivalent if they are the same or equal

equivalent fraction equivalent fractions are equal fractions. Example: $\frac{1}{2} = \frac{2}{4} = \frac{3}{6}$

estimate is like a good guess

even chance if an event has an even chance, there is the same chance of it happening as not happening

face the flat side of a solid shape

factor a number that will divide exactly into other numbers. Example: 5 is a factor of 20

formula a formula (plural is formulae) uses letters or words to give a rule

frequency the number of times that something happens is called the frequency

highest common factor the greatest whole number that divides exactly into two or more other numbers

horizontal a horizontal line is a straight level line across, in the same direction as the horizon

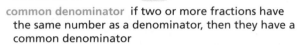

lowest common multiple the lowest number that is a multiple of two or more numbers

mean this is the total divided by the number of items. So the mean of 3, 1, 6 and 2 is (3 + 1 + 6 + 2) ÷ 4 = 3

median the middle number in an ordered list. Example: 3, 8, 11, 15, 16. The median number is 11

mode the most common number in a list. Example: 2, 6, 4, 2, 5, 5, 2. The mode is 2

multiple a multiple is a number made by multiplying together two other numbers

negative number a number less than zero on the number line

net the net of a 3D shape is what it looks like when it is opened out flat

numerator the top number of a fraction. Example: $\frac{3}{5}$

parallel lines that are parallel always stay the same distance apart and never meet

partition break numbers up into their place values. Example: 476 = 400 + 70 + 6

percentage this is a fraction out of 100, shown with a % sign

perpendicular a perpendicular line is one that is at right angles to another line

prime factor any factor that is a prime number is a prime factor

prime number a prime number only has two factors, 1 and itself. For example, 23 is a prime number as it can only be divided exactly by 1 and 23

probability scale an ordered line numbered from 0, which is the probability of an impossible event, to 1, which is the probability of a certain event. All probabilities lie between 0 and 1

proportion this is the same as finding the fraction of the whole amount. Example: the proportion of red cubes is 3 out of 5, or $\frac{3}{5}$

protractor a tool for measuring angles

quadrant one quarter of a circle. Also the name given to each of the four quarters on a coordinates grid or graph

quotient this is the number of times that one number will divide into another. Example: when you divide 18 by 3, the quotient is 6

ratio this compares one amount with another. Example: the ratio of red cubes to blue cubes is 3:2

remainder if a number cannot be divided exactly by another number, then there is a whole number answer with an amount left over, called a remainder

sequence a list of numbers which usually have a pattern. They are often numbers written in order

square number numbers multiplied by themselves make square numbers. Example: 4 × 4 = 16. The first five square numbers are 1, 4, 9, 16 and 25

square root the opposite of a square number. A number, when multiplied by itself, makes a square number. Example: the square root of 25 is 5

symmetry when two halves of a shape or pattern are identical

vertical a line that is straight up or down, at right angles to a horizontal line

vertices (single is vertex) the corners of a 3D shape, where edges meet